The Better Part of Some Time

The Better Part of Some Time

Mike Madill

First Edition

A 2021 Don Gutteridge Poetry Award Winner

Wet Ink Books
www.WetInkBooks.com
WetInkBooks@gmail.com

The Better Part of Some Time
by Mike Madill

Cover Image – Shutterstock.com
Cover Design – Richard M. Grove
Layout and Design – Richard M. Grove
Author Bio Photo – Lisa Burkhardt

Typeset in Garamond
Printed and bound in Canada
Distributed in USA by Ingram,
        – to set up an account – 1-800-937-0152

Library and Archives Canada Cataloguing in Publication

Title: The better part of some time / Mike Madill.
Other titles: Better part of sometime
Names: Madill, Mike, author.
Description: Poems.
Identifiers: Canadiana 20220203628 | ISBN 9781989786642 (softcover)
Classification: LCC PS8626.A325 B48 2022 | DDC C811/.6—dc23

We gaze into the night
as if remembering the bright unbroken planet
we once came from,
to which we will never
be permitted to return.
We are amazed how hurt we are.
We would give anything for what we have.

Tony Hoagland, 'Jet'

For Dad,
whose love of language knew no bounds,
and will always inspire me.

For Lisa,
whose love of laughter and all things sweet
reminds me every day of the light.

And for Barry,
who believed in me long before I did.

Tether

Blue sky broken
by sweep of thistle-down,
smattering of seeds,
windblown, restless.
Every blink a freeze-frame,
tethering befores and afters.
An endless rope-ladder
flung into the unknown.

Cling to the belief
of safety in numbers,
like shoaling fish or
flocking birds.
Keep each other in sight,
cherish that tenuous grasp
amidst the tidal drift
of everything unnamed.

Infinity's a hard thing to bear –
traversing its blind expanse,
no point to the horizon
without camel or compass.
The merciless stretch of too many
summits, too much to bury.
No guarantee
a soul won't spill
instead of float.

Contents

1. Little Voice

2. The Ricochet of Sky

3. Solar Flare

I

Little Voice

To raise the veil.
To see what you're saying goodbye to.

Louise Gluck, 'Averno'

Red

I listened to every quavery word.
More than once, he peered through me
and warned: *Don't get old.*
Face grizzled with white stubble,
shoulders stooped, the slant
of his tweed cap. His gnarled hand would rise
from the post-and-wire fence between us,
give my shoulder a cold pat.
He showed me which tall shoots of grass to chew.
I followed suit, a bittersweet taste
to summer I never questioned.

I remember the day I watched
from behind Mom's ruffled kitchen curtains
as he shuffled to his sacred garden's edge,
raised his rifle at the corn-raiding raccoon
bristling and brazen in the hot sun.
It jerked with the bang,
its sudden sag felt deep
inside my ribs.

Gone to clean his gun, he phoned
to give the all-clear. Mom let me hop the fence
to see my first wild animal up close
before he returned with a shovel.
She made me promise not to touch it
but never warned how death would rush up
with bared teeth, eyes clouding, staring back
from behind a gritty, black mask.
Blood red lay splattered across
half-eaten cobs scattered in the dirt.

The grackles and jays resumed,
the far spruces shaking off their
shadows, but I failed to find anything
that hadn't lost its golden glow.
Everywhere, crimson undercurrents,
scarlet threads weaving through
fresh-cut grass. They circled
our rusted burn-barrel, swirled around
our Datsun's radio antenna, stained
the walls of my childhood home.
The inevitable eleventh hour lurking
within, poised to spill its reckoning.
Glint of a trigger, white of an eye,
a young stalk of timothy uprooted,
chewed, then spit out.

Origin Unknown

The photo doubly exposed –
a dark ring encircling my head
like an astronaut's helmet.

Back to terra firma, reacquaint
with the strangely new again,
sun in my eyes,

wagon barely made for one.
I fancied it mine, wooden
gunwales digging in-

to my legs, little brother's back
heavy against my chest.
(Steve almost a year –

hard-soled baby shoes.
My sneakers flat on the ground,
proof I was invincible at three.)

Mom towing us around
the bumpy yard by the handle.
The wagon nothing more

than a shallow-sided wooden tray
atop a metal webbing of bars
and channels for axles and such,

coloured red to feel faster.

Flash of Blue

Despite the call to sit up straight,
I slump in front of
the stone fireplace, fretting
over my latest math test,
ankle still throbbing
from bike crash, wondering
how much the blue flash bulb
will blind me this time.

When will I once again
be in trouble for pestering
my little brother in the car,
forgetting to shovel the walk
before dinner, or talking
during the six o'clock news?

Will Monday's school bus
be full of bullies?
Will my teacher scar me
with a C? Can I disappear
into the furthest corner of the room?
If I close my eyes, will the picture
take shape without me?

Shutterbug

The ice-blue flash of my new
Kodak Instamatic slices the gloom,
glint of winter sun through taffeta
curtains, bleary as week-old butter.
Mom's at the kitchen counter,
hands suspended mid-slice
over the cutting board, slate-blue
cardigan drooping from the weight
of late afternoon, cluttered
drying-rack draped with
canary-yellow dish-gloves.

To her right, the Osterizer blender,
cabinet-mounted AM radio, chrome
toaster threatening to out-glare.
To her left, my collie Prince,
head at hip-height, ready for spills.
The nearest cupboard door hangs ajar,
revealing my brother's and my plastic cups,
two stacks of orange and red.

I don't know why I took the shot, or if
I was grounded after being told not to.
None of it comes back quite like
the certainty of a scolding. Another
Christmas gone. Shutterbug son
with 24 frames to fill – the hunch
of her shoulders, set of her mouth,
the shame of an ear stuck between
strands of housework hair.

Da Capo

In my holiday best, I'm perched
on a stool by our console TV,
music stand never high enough
to block their stares, Segovia scary
as ever. I'm displayed like a stag's head,
the wall behind me adorned with Mom's
twirling anniversary clock, Dad's revered
sharpshooter plaques. *Smile*, they urge,
as if I'm currency, making this show
even more a sham. Three etudes in,
my fingers stumble on the strings,
Mom shakes her head, a grim *No*.
I begin again.

In Dry Dock

On creaky porch stairs, my brother
and I cuddle up to Granny B..
She pulls us in close and Grandad snaps
the moment, her hair the perfect perm,
a careful smile for the camera.

Front and centre, the relentless stretch
of my skinny, white legs. I'm sporting
a logo-less blue jersey, its bold *61*
unclaimed. Steve's, a faceless
burnt orange, matches the front shutters.

Fiddlehead ferns bustle and brim
along the front walk, leading
to a young hosta in a tall, clay planter,
like a phoenix hatchling born from soot.

Behind us, Grandad's bow-rider
nestles on its trailer, poised
for Georgian Bay, Evinrude outboard
beefy as a wrestler.

Deep in the late-afternoon shadows
lurks the neighbour's insulbrick,
lake-blue shingles hazed over
with the amber of pine needles.

The screen door yawns,
Granny makes orange soda floats
and we try once again
to beat her at Rummy, praying
Grandad will launch the boat.

But he fritters away the day
in the garage, rummaging around
for that certain wrench, waylaid
by the lopsidedness
of his own crooked shelves.

Later, we spot him spinning a yarn
to a huddle of neighbours, beers
all around. We set the table for Granny,
battered aluminum pots bubbling
on the burners, place her favourite tea cup

with its wild English roses by her plate,
Grandad's mug a utilitarian green.
She gets us to call him home
a third time. By then, he's confounded
why she didn't work her magic

to keep the roast warm and tender
for his arrival. He eats
heartily, though, promises
he'll take us out fishing
tomorrow,
just like yesterday.

Grandfather's Garage

Twisted t-bar posts, rusted water pumps,
fan motors long since expired.
Brand new brake rotors
for a '93 Windstar, pitch forks,
peony rings, coils of compressor hose.
Beneath thick blankets of sawdust

and grime, stacks of fridge capacitors,
gallon-jugs of two-stroke engine oil,
corded drills and saws strictly off-limits
to a younger me. Benches cluttered
with greasy wrenches, vises, ratchets –
a blur of other gadgets I couldn't name.

Tucked away on a corner shelf,
the popsicle-maker we built together
for my grade seven science fair, wedged
between a tangle of fishing rods and
his trusty tackle-box, dented and packed
with lost summers' lures and hooks.

Indelible

He stares out the window, grey of rain
in his eyes, squeezes his walker's handles
a little tighter. More of a chair
than a means to get anywhere, handy for
unloading the dishwasher or
peeling potatoes at the sink. Eighty-six and
alone, Grandad's taught himself to cook –
pork tenderloin, fistful of baby carrots.

He asks what my brother's been up to,
hasn't seen him since the funeral,
where more than Granny B. died;
all of us a little less now
that we've been handed over to memories,
like the Humpty-Dumpty chips shaken
into two Tupperware bowls;
games of Rummy well past our bedtime;
Granny tucking us in-
to our shared bed at the cottage.

Solitude steeps here,
no less than the stains
the cat left behind the couch.
Some marks don't come out, indelible
as two grad photos tilting
across faded wallpaper, black-gowned
grandsons avoiding each other's gaze.

Breakaway

for Steve

Skates slung from shouldered
hockey stick, stubborn trudge
through miles of powder,
little brother in tow.
Worn out from times-tables,
provincial capitals, Louis Riel and
his Red River brigade.

Distant shots thunder off the boards
of the outdoor rink. *The big kids,*
the lean-to's bench strewn
with parkas, sloppy skidoo boots,
a few empty Exports. I double-check
my brother's laces, wobble with him to
the smaller rink, but shots clanging
off goal-posts finally goad me
up to the bigger ice. I let go of
Steve's hand, leave him
leaning hard on his stick.

No one tells me whose side I'm on.
I swivel back and forth between
imaginary blue lines, within
reach of the boards, like a dog-paddler
hugging the shore. The lone tomboy,
Joanne, slides me a soft pass, but it's
scooped up by some hatless hotshot,
my brother taking it all in.

Spotting his solitary teeter,
she dekes around me, tosses him a
fresh puck from her pocket.
With Grade 2 gusto, he swats away
the one I left behind,
(with carved initials), straight into
a snowbank, stick raised high.

Fraught

And so I sit, beside the other
grandmother, the one in the city
we visit on birthdays and Christmas,
trips fraught with Dad's chain-smoking.

She hauls me in too close, the dark
green daubs on her dress
like the olives I've
never been able to stomach.

I'm snagged by her '60's holdover
horn-rims, the brocade couch's sheen,
my wince of a grin outdone
by her fake camera-smile.

She tears open her gift-wrapped
Vera Lynn LP in record time, mutters
Didn't you get me this last year?

House Arrest

The walls are crooked
with portraits of the living,
though Grammy M. attracts
spirits as well – more
of an ease with the dead.
She never notices
the curtains sagging, broadloom
balding, or doesn't care, leaves me
feeling smeared as a butter-dish
buried beneath the table clutter.
She prefers a brooding sky.
Half-deaf, spine crumbling,
what some might call
a kind of house arrest.
But she's completely at home
with her paranoia, money stashed
in wrinkled paperbacks, under
couch cushions. Cheeks
superficially powdered,
no more need for touch-ups –
this is who she is
in the wreckage of family photos.

The Other Side

Though Church-of-England raised,
she believed *in the beyond*
of other lives – even called
a medium by some. But did she receive
a message of her own death,
(suffocation by scrambled eggs
four months short of a hundred),
or was she stunned like us?

I last saw Grammy M. three days before
she died, her grip still strong, no hint of
the frailty to come, no apparent end
to the saga. When she left us
feeling mortal, the crude semi-circle
shifted from hospital room to graveside,
gathered in wrinkled suits and ties,
the women's high heels sinking
in spring sod, the city's white noise
wafting down long rows of tombstones,
a ceaseless static.

At Dad's insistence, his bottom lip quivering,
I thrust the shovel into wet earth
but failed to hold it steady. It tipped
without me, unprepared
for the echo of its thump.

Jesus and the Soap-Dish

Our first house together was barely
seven hundred square feet, with a soap-dish
too fancy for it – an eight-inch high mermaid,
ivory-coloured porcelain, tail curled
around the bowl. I gave in once,
and with a sudsy thumb and finger
wiped clean one of her pointed breasts,
small as a grape.

My grandmother's bathroom was locked
in the '50's with pepto-pink walls,
black and white tiles checkering the floor.
The medicine cabinet door never stayed closed,
chrome trim rusted with age-spots.
The sink's ledge barely had room for her
toothbrush and Crest, balding facecloth
always draped over the edge.

I dreaded going in there, facing her
slimy soap-dish, brass filigree. I'd pry free
the bar soaked mushy from the tray shared with
her partial denture. I never touched this
mechanical part of Grammy M.,
fearing I'd catch something by grazing the hook-
and-wire, its three teeth bucking up
at the crooked vanity light,
bulbs dusty enough to have brush-cuts.

The basin had separate hot and cold handles
like stylized Maltese crosses, reminding me
of her Lord's picture in the living room
opposite her favourite chair.
It was a somber sepia portrait,
long hair tangled with woven thorns,
eyes shadowed and closed.
One day she smiled, told me to take
a closer look – his eyes appeared open,
peering at me – a painter's spooky trick.
I wound up with the picture
when everyone else steered clear, unable
to wash their hands of it quick enough.

Smother

My folks talked of the time
they bundled my brother and I
into the car, chased down
massive black plumes
mushrooming high on the horizon.
A barn ablaze, neighbours gathering,
hands on hips –
dazzled dumb by flames.
Unable to turn the channel, I bawled
in the back seat until finally home in bed –
hot anguish heavy on my small bones.

Like my grown-up fear
of coming home to fire trucks,
house engulfed.
Freud would waggle his
finger, suggest something mother-ish,
Jung mull over a new *arsonist* archetype.
Maybe I was burned
at the stake in another life.
A friend pointed out my collection
of antique fire extinguishers:
polished copper with plates of
stamped brass, tall tubes of sand,
and the early aerosols,
those shaving-foam frauds.

I think of the night we hosted a fondue,
waves of heat rising up
from the burner like a blue cobra
flicking its tongue.
Three sides of the table were laughing,
sipping chardonnay while the creature
lured me in. Soon, it would be
running riot across the table, wrapping
itself around my throat, choking me
on childhood smoke.

Finding a Face

for Vivian

She'd stopped teaching English
at my high school long before
I stepped off the bus.
I painted her window-frames, laid
floor tile, fixed a sticky door.
She gushed over my poetry,
her eyes lighting up as she
pored over my words like
they were Byron's or Blake's,
part of me staring down
at my shoelaces, the rest of me
dashing through her screen door.
Emphysema and phlebitis kept her
stuck most days in a slatted chair,
ashtray blossoming
like an artichoke, desk-lamp glaring
over Formica and the *Globe and Mail.*
She brandished a sturdy magnifying glass,
extracted from my lines things I hadn't seen,
vowed to make my upcoming reading.
But from the stage I failed to find her
amongst the caps and hairdos,
pictured her dozing in front
of her seventeen-inch Zenith.
She broke her promise
to call me back come fall
for more odd jobs, more poems,
but my follow-up might've looked
like I was fishing for fresh praise.
Baseboarding her neighbour's bedrooms
in February, I asked after her.
She's gone, he said. *A stroke, I think.*
I heard her voice, her smoker's laugh,
but couldn't conjure up the place inside
where I'd hidden her face.

Strut

for John

A wavery hello, as if a weak connection.
Mary tells me she'll pass along my
birthday wishes to John. Eighty-three,
abruptly bedridden, no strength for bluster
and strut, evenings sweeping in like oil spills.

> *Tell me again about the summer*
> *you built a basement underneath*
> *your fieldstone homestead*
> *with nothing more than trusses,*
> *shovels and will.*

I kick myself for thinking of him in the past tense.
I wish he'd pick up the bedroom phone,
tell me it's only 5:30
and why the hell am I home so early,
bitch about the TV cable
he fished through the wall
the other day, before he was laid low.

But instead, it's only Mary recounting
the ambulance ride, seven hours
stuck in Emerg., mystery prescription,
specialist's appointment in July.

What about all those years of hefting furnaces
up flights of stairs, jostling six-by-sixes
and load-bearing beams – still no framework
to brace shifting, settling bones.

I picture him gripping an eyelet-trimmed duvet
with those gnarled hands, staring
at the tedious ceiling, listening to his wife
do all the talking.

Evening Sun

after Louise Gluck's 'Widows'

My great-aunt Elva's house
peels paint like sunburnt skin.
Window-boxes listing,
eavestroughs bristling
with maple-key sprouts,
everything shabbier now
beside the big, new Buick
Uncle Reg would never buy.

The screen door's leaping deer,
singed ash-white by years of
evening sun, gives way to
a stale whiff of mothballs and
Old Spice. Floors buckling, walls
faded to a malignant green.
Unheard-of second cups of Red Rose
after the eleven o'clock news
linger like an indulgence.

No, she can no longer
roll her eyes at his
plaid-shirted back or the way
his shredded Kleenex kept
sabotaging the wash; no one else
to double-check the doors at night,
floodlight flicked on for company
before creaking up the stairs.

And yet, her arthritic fingers
sometimes hesitate on the bureau
before bed, where his ill-fitting
dentures would grin,
setting overnight in dried spit;
when she'd almost begrudge the dark
and the strangeness of his faltering
Love you, too.

Flying Solo

for Mom

She cut the cheque winter before last,
finally buying into a gated community
like her and Dad often dreamed.

He'd be proud of her: pantry stocked
from Winn-Dixie, plates and pots
from yard sales and thrift shops.

But would he have managed the same resolve
if she'd gone first, or only eaten from cans,
wearing out the microwave and TV?

The elegance of Spanish moss sweeps
away a snowbird's chill. Pea-sized acorns
ping off the lanai's tin roof, where vertical blinds

surrender to morning sun with a squeal.
Lately, her gray is emerging with a grace
that can't be bottled. Friends knock

and let themselves in, she coaxes their terriers
up on the couch beside her.
She sets aside her Sudoku or crossword

to tag along to the flea market or local
wildlife sanctuary, grabbing her floppy sun-hat
from the table, a bite to eat along the way.

A different mother sewed the name tags
into all our little clothes, laid out Sunday roasts,
hosted spelling bees. I had to ask to be excused

from the dinner table, my homework solved before TV,
rules and manners remembered under searing stares,
time-outs, the occasional wooden spoon.

Her table and counter stayed spotless;
carrots and onions in her garden kept
perfect roll-call rows; every slice of bread

and cookie accounted for. But gone now is the
clothespin pinch, the grim set of her mouth
to meet another day. Learning the lawn doesn't thrive

here, she pays a guy to worry about it for her.
She'll pick a spot behind the carport
for a pineapple plant, then watch it grow.

II

The Ricochet of Sky

I put my arms around a trunk and squeezed it,
then I lay down on my father's grave.

Sharon Olds, 'One Year'

Deadfall

An ATV has grooved the ground ahead,
tread-chunked snow shaped like
Shinto temples, the path's spine
a phantom deadfall draped
in death-shroud white, pock-marks
like dirty begging bowls.

Saplings lean into their weave above,
snowflakes scattering.
It's easier for branches to reach out
in woods unnamed, without the need
of a father.

The world was safer when
I thought he was king of the oaks.
But now, days darken sooner,
sucked November-bare.
A shadowed stump surrenders
to tenacious moss.

Squinting

Tendrils of incense
snake upwards like
Dad's cigarette smoke,
cozying around me.

Alone one day by his ashtray,
I unbent one of the butts, pinched
it between finger and thumb.
Sour, woody taste on my tongue.
Squinting
because I'd watched him squint.

Mother caught me,
had one of her conniptions.

Made me wonder
why grown-ups needed
canned laughter, corked joy,
cartons of Viscount
from the corner counter
of our local IGA.

Keeping my world inside the lines
so I wouldn't become that kid
beside me in Sunday school
adorning disciples in his Bible-book
with horns and goatees,
cigarette dangling from Jesus' lips.

Ricochet

Dad's cool radiates
beside me, fresh-faced little sentry
leaning against his hip with
checkered pants and wide-tie dreams,
my belt slung loose, gunslinger-style.
His cuffs rolled up, big hand
draped over my bony shoulder.
Behind him, an ashtray
the death-knell no one could hear.
The first malignancy
nearly leveled him at forty-nine,
but those hands, even after
all their wasting, still big enough
to shelter me from the ricochet of sky.

Sixteen Clocks

Dad's silent workshop, milling machine
looming in cluttered gloom, bleeds of
shaved metal long since swept away.

Spare engine for his 240Z
listing south, its rebuild no longer
postponed, but cancelled. CD player
for the Firebird still in the box.
By the workbench, discarded coveralls,
grubby next to shiny clusters of keys
hung by their broken necks.

Finding the tool I need, I shut the door
behind me, just as he pulls up
on his candy-red scooter.
I've been meaning to get to that
for the better part of some time.
A Tilley hat shades his bifocals
as he watches me climb the ladder,
installing his new closed-circuit camera
under the eaves. The system's monitor
is placed on the end-table, within reach
of the glider rocker, where he sits
trying to re-set his watch to one
of sixteen clocks in the house.

His hands, puffy from steroids, clutch
the handrail I fit alongside his bed,
grab the bar beside his raised toilet,
fumble for his beloved bottle
of Percocet.

Single-Handed

How was it you appeared
years younger – *healthier* –
the second-last time
I saw you? It was the old you
again, cracking jokes,
pulling your Crazy Guggenheim
face at us in our Isolation gowns.

In the night-table drawer
your shaving kit went untouched,
hearing aids tucked
in the side pouch. But still
you heard it coming, that
ethereal express.

Every time I left you
that summer I'd look back, find you
high up, waving from behind
tinted glass. How the hell you made it
from bed to windowsill
single-handed, I'll never know.

Freight Train

*"That you died in fear and pain
is fear and pain and that you lived
is life to me." – from Ursula K. LeGuin's 'You, Her, I'.*

Pick a diagnosis –
chances are he had it.
Not that it's a question
of what's earned, good or bad,
but, Jesus, such an unfair
array of pills and procedures.
Pointless to even try
rhyming off all his burdens.
Besides, *it's nobody's
damn business,* he always said.

Covering his contorted face
with my hands would've been
an act so close to smothering
I couldn't bear the thought.
But his features finally softened
after the coup-de-grâce heart attack –
our last kick in the gut, shared.
He's resting now really meant
*We brought him back
so you could say goodbye.*

I used to think he could outrun
the freight trains that rumbled
behind our house, hauling loads of
lumber and shiny new vehicles bound
for other worlds.
Countless tankers, too, brimming
with diesel, sulfur and chlorine,
like his own medley of chemicals:
potassium held in check, blood sugar
steadied, immunity suppressed.
Everything it took to keep him
upright, if not alert; alive
one more hour.

In Pencil

Long after midnight, I picked my way
through Saturday's crossword, reciting
every clue like a poem.

17- Across: Where do elephants
go to die? Four letters. *Away*. Or
maybe *Home*. *Gone* is too much, too
profane. All I could do was watch your life
unmooring. The final insult:
disposable cloaks of gowns and gloves,
last touch denied.

1- Down. Still no clue.
68 - Across:
I'd like to change *Destiny* to
Forever, another seven-
letter word.

Lingering has weakness to it,
a submission that wasn't your style.
Instead, you made a swift job of it,
eluding (6 - Down) the code blue.
Technique is found in your follow-through,
you used to say. They managed to restart
your heart, but I suspect you were
already thick in the swim of silence.

Personal Effects

1. Bedside

Two nurses grimly lift the hem of your
blue bed sheet, denying my view of the
doctor removing your intubation tube.
Then, I see your chapped lips, slightly parted,
poised with an unfinished thought.

Your eyelids are only half-closed, revealing
white under the left, the right still
crimson from a fall three days ago.
They found you fetal on the floor, midway
between bed and toilet,

a corner of your blanket dragged
off the bed, draped over your shoulder.
This bloody cornea is like a rage
you'd never shown before,
dashing our final superhero hopes.

Without the breathing tube, he might last
five minutes, an hour at most.
Your chest rises and falls in an almost
imperceptible way, and I can't help
but steal a shameful glance at the clock

high on the wall behind me. Your warm hand,
your grip less than I need. The grit of
pain held so close for so long. Fear of failure,
regret for never cutting ties with your toxic mother,
the relentless pressure to provide.

I stare at your chest, willing it to rise
just once more. Outside the ground-floor window,
souls mill about the parking lot. No one
has drawn the curtains and the November dusk
tumbles in.

2. Oil Can

At the visitation, two picture boards
on easels, riddled with snaps scrambled
together. Nearby, a display table
I'm prouder for having assembled.

Trophies from target-shooting
tournaments; Robert Service poems and
Shakespeare's *Hamlet* tempered by a dog-eared
volume of bawdy limericks; one of your
precision micrometers propped beside
a trusty, seven-pound sledge. *The degree*
of finesse depends on the job.

Front and centre, your beloved oil can.
Sporting a chipped, red finish, its pint-sized,
cylindrical reservoir doubles as
the handle behind a trigger lever
and slender neck-to-nozzle. You yearned to
rid your world of rust and squeaks. If it turned,
twisted, pivoted or rolled, watch out.

A friend takes special interest in the
table's oily centerpiece. I regale her
with your 10W30 crusade,
startled by the stretch of my own smile and how
easily a lump slips into my throat.

3. Toiletry Bag

In less than 48 hours, the
hospital calls, requesting I collect
your personal effects.
I stand at the nursing station,
within sight of the room that was yours.

Night before last, our family owned
that end of Critical Care, its hallway
solemn and somber and stopped. But now,
business as usual: orderlies bustling,
ringtones vying, the P.A. blaring
its latest call-to-arms.

A yellow mop bucket loiters outside
the nearest semi-private ward, its
caretaker banging the walls with
exaggerated swoops, backing
his busy way out the door.

A nurse asks why I'm here.
My own voice manages
For my Dad's things.
Across her counter she hands me
a small, sad smile and
a faceless, clear bag of your last clothes.

Later, I force myself to untwist the knot,
unwrap this final *you*: the sensible,
black loafers you were convinced someone
tried to steal the first night, a pair of
navy blue track pants you never
recovered enough to try on,
the matching, button-up cardigan
Mom sent along with good intentions.

Nestled further down, your toiletry bag.
A black, unremarkable pouch
containing your loyal electric razor,
a simple comb (with two gray hairs),
a white-and-blue, much-abused Oral-B
toothbrush and a half-pack of Hall's
lozenges, (mentho-lyptus flavor).

In the side pocket, your hearing aids with
surprisingly few traces of wax.
This is as close as I can get,
yet not nearly enough. I cradle them
in my hands but still need more proof
you were just here, that the distance
between us hasn't exploded,
irrevocable and out of reach.

Crosshairs

Tucked away in a file folder,
I find a batch of your top scores —
nearly all in the high nineties —

complete with copious notes
how to improve focus, control
breath, a more patient trigger pull.

So much lead we shot down-range,
aiming for pinwheels, *possibles*,
even your praise.

But now I'm fresh out of vision,
crosshairs won't come clear.
You've added so much distance

beyond our twenty-five-yard
paper targets, marksmanship
too superhuman to match.

Timing, stance, grip.
Then another kickback of grief,
worse than any .38 calibre flinch.

Shop-Coat

I try on one of your shop-coats –
your hands used to emerge
from these same cuffs, only beefier.

Snug across the shoulders, short
in the sleeves, as though you're
telling me to go buy my own.

All I smell is grease and oil.
Was there ever a time you worried
whether I'd succeed?

This latest *Happy Birthday*
more dirge than ode.

If only you could know me now –
blue eyes bleary, fear
grinding its teeth, loss a Goliath
we might have shared.

Shards

Seven shirt buttons,
seven holes. Don't get me started
on socks and shoes. Belt cinched,
wearing thin the habits of time.

End-tables too big for my
new space, shins bruised,
back clenched in spasm again.

Walls lined with shelves
of good intentions,
or maybe, good intentions
shelved.

Pill bottles tucked out of sight
re-emerge. Keys for a changed lock,
windowsills on which to rest my chin,
chimney smoke familiar shapes.

Apple worms like heirlooms.
Oh, the vacant stares, floors swept
too much, never leaving anything un-
disturbed.

Staying Vertical

An early night would have been smart, but
cards and Jack Daniels crept up on me.
Now, it's nearly nine and I'm staring down
grogginess in the mirror, stubbled chin,
jaw bracing for the echo of coffee
and bagel to come, a couple of pills
and a hefty Pepto slug.

At the trailhead, I do my best
to brave friends' good-natured jeers:
never having traipsed the Nokiidaa Trail
before, the same sad stature
as not keeping up with the latest Thai place,
or visiting the McMichael Gallery since '09.
Even a neglected throng of aspen chime in,
or am I over-reacting?

Staying vertical might very well be
my only accomplishment today.
Everyone else's notebooks and pens poised
for details make this poets' walk seem
insurmountable, as out of reach
as the wild-apple dangle overhead.

I'm unable to forget myself, nature
too wild and deep to wade into.
Harvest hues overwhelm,
too vivid to bear; an ash leaf
of freckled yellow glows
like an overripe pear; a goldenrod's
leaf opts for burgundy.
For one excruciating moment,
a kestrel glides overhead, keening
through leafless tree-tops, delivering
a silence I had to hear.

Little Xs

If I thought it would help
through all the chaos,
I'd take up smoking
your leftover Viscounts, drag deep
on one cigarette after another,
until my horizon leveled out.
The time you'd take
putting time on hold for a spell.

You only confessed
one of your dreams to me –
archaeological digs in Egypt,
buried long ago.
But you never shared your fears.
What a gift it would've been
to learn you were broken, too.

That black dog keeps a bead on me,
always yapping how disjointed
and incapable I am,
overwhelmed and overlooked,
squandering
the degree that hung
in the hallway I used to own.

There's something to be said
for asylums – three meals a day,
a prescribed numbness to shuffle
through the calendar, little Xs
creeping across the weeks
until the flip of another month
renews false hope.

Would standing in the rain
rid me of worry, drench the last
of my loss? No sangfroid,
no faith in the future. Break my legs.
Wrap them around my neck,
if that's the price and pose it takes.

All Over Again

Quit finding new ways to leave
me. Losing you over and over
doesn't mean I love you any less,
just that it's dulled the burn a bit.

It was after my eulogy for Granny B.
I remember you finally
declaring you were proud of me.
A limo ride I keep reliving –
you facing forward, me looking
back at you.

Today, someone new will need
to be told you've passed away:
dentist, podiatrist, osteopath –
naïve, perky calls
I wonder will ever be
finished stirring the space
you used to hold.

Even myself, pausing
in your shop's doorway,
half-expecting you
to shimmer into view.

Recalibrate

1. Losing

It's 3 AM but your body doesn't care
about the calendar or the clock.
You cling to my arms
as hard as I clutch yours. Heavier,
despite the dropped pounds.
Your hair now a disheveled crown.
I lift you up, you get wiped down.
Face to face, yet no glance shared.

2. Lost

No manuals for custom tools to
work copper, brass, cold-rolled
steel; no clue how to recalibrate
the hoist, re-light the pilot, reset your air
compressor. No back-stories
for complicated prototypes.
Another April since you turned
away, locked the door behind you.
Hard to copy what's harder to conjure:
blueprint-wiring, spot-less welds,
table-saw science. Someday,
I'll finally earn your chainsaw poise.

Six Feet Up

I sold your car hoist today, watched it
trundle out of here strapped to a hay-wagon,
silhouette of its four corner posts jutting up
into the late afternoon haze like rib-bones.
Come winter, the new owner's Model A
will be warm and dry and six feet up
in a Quonset hut. I still see you
working the levers, ever on guard
for glitches. You should've lived longer.

You logged a lot of miles
in the early days, installing
TV transmitter towers from Inuvik to
Antigonish, left with little time
to help raise a couple of sons who turned out
less like you than maybe you'd hoped.

I've chosen words, arranging the gizmos
of every de facto tear-down and rebuild
in my head. And yet, words, too,
don't always mesh, like the stripped teeth
of gears. I approach the real you, as though
laying down paving stones, page by page.

My Father Meets Up with God Again

I imagine God waiting
for my father, decked out in
well-worn leather jacket, rugged
work jeans, buckled biker boots.

The oft-purported review
of one's life: did Dad once more
clutch the ache of an empty stomach,
flinch from the shivering vise across

his shoulders when his mother ran
out of coal? Did he lose his wits
all over again from welts
criss-crossing his back,

hear jumbled shouts as she was
wrenched away before beating him
into oblivion with
the buckle end of a belt?

Did he clench his greasy hands, inhale
again the black scent of dirty oil,
reliving his first tune-up
at 14, on a '48

Plymouth? Did his lips tingle from
re-kissing his new bride, his
knees wobbly as they reached
Irazu's summit a second time?

So much buoyancy and bitterness,
then those painful final years of
spinal stenosis. Picture God throwing
him a Sam Elliott smirk,

leather creaking as He raises
an arm to give Dad a re-
assuring slap on the back.
It's over now, God says,

maybe pulling a pack of smokes
from His pocket – another time's
sure and steady brotherly gesture.
Their shared, easy silence:

God happily puffing away,
Dad drawing deep
on the irony of it all, marveling
at how much he'd missed this, never

tasted one so good.

Ballast

after M.E. Sparks' 'Afterimage', 2016

Two navy-blue coffins stacked
to save space. The top holds
what would've been
the remains of my father.
The bottom one I call home.

It has no place to peek out
at the life around me, no means of
anyone or anything gaining entry.
I breathe the same recycled air,
less apt to betray me, take solace
in the darkness. When I feel up to it,
I feed on that same darkness, so it can't
always be feeding on me.

Above me rests a dependency
I never expected. Navy blue should evoke
boundless ocean expanse, not a weighty bolt
of altar cloth. He hasn't uttered a word
in six years now, yet I still find ways
to judge myself on his behalf.

Deep Light

You should've sent me rain
enough to be worthy of Noah,
worthy of you.
Who would've thought
the intricacies of drowning
could gather light so deep?
Why couldn't it have rained
the day you died, instead of
the studded strap of sunlight?
The rotting of one more rainbow
growing rank, no one left
to share the secrets of manhood.
Even more flickering down
through pine boughs, spilling
into the skylight. The weight
of other people's dawns
above me, their blinding light
the blistering stares of
jury and judge. Front-room
afternoons heating up
without the turn of a page.
No clouds to follow,
to find my way back
to a surface I no longer trust.

Alive

Were you scared, too?
You could've
said so – not confession, more
connection. *The things we do*
just to keep ourselves alive:
your opiate bluster, our swirl
of post-hospital hopes.

The distances reined in, all
the fences half-standing. How
you appeared to persevere.

Does this sound like blame? Dying
is the last chance to be ourselves.

Beyond the drudgery: showers,
leftovers, creaky knees,
waiting for the alarm to shake
the rigor mortis off. Every
sunbeam revealing even light
is made of dust.

Oh, to have one more round with
you, hold you close
to my chest. I want you back, so I
can punch you, kiss you.
Your empty chair
now everything
I'll never master.

III

Solar Flare

Just because we have birds inside us,
we don't have to be cages.

Dean Young, 'Instant Recognition Between Strangers'

Night Crossing

after Pablo Neruda's 'A Small Animal'

Watch midnight scrape clean
the astral ruins of day: spectral cries
of release; the breathless wash.

Who wouldn't choose to die in the night?

Float high above apple orchards,
fruit blurring, barely green; incessant
rivers, darkest dark sweeping the sky.

Tilled fields like furrowed brows,
cynics ever dismissing dreamers.

Embrace the blackness,
squeeze until the light
bursts from pores
and the fear of falling
falls away.

Retreat

A bona fide fixer-upper,
propped on posts above Otter Lake's
granite shore, hunter-green
plywood and planks posing as *cottage*,
switch-back stairway teetering
down to the water's edge.

Inside, relic of a harvest-gold stove,
crooked kitchen cupboards harbouring
mouse-shit and mismatched plates.
Dinner lurking in the fridge
amidst my friend's infantry of beer,
a mangled pack of pizza-pops,
some expired half-and-half cream.

The last of my meal dabbed into
a swizzle of cold ketchup.
Black-water bath off the end of the dock.
After dark, nameless bugs flutter
in my flashlight beam while I'm
camped in the outhouse,
half expecting the crash of a bear.

I unroll my sleeping bag
over the sway-backed sofa-bed
steeped in cigarette smoke,
try dreaming myself clean.
But I'm cast away in reclusive waters,
car keys bunched in my pocket
like a rosary, not the Thoreau
I'd hoped to be.

Immersion

for Barry

I prayed for no problems in the city,
my car complaining more now
than it used to, nagging
warning lights marring the dash.
You tell me to turn right, then left
at the next lights, now try and sneak over
to that other lane, my windows motion-
smeared. There's less room to think
here, less time to breathe –
urban full-immersion.
Spaces crushed into slices of alleyway.
Bloor and College Streets with the same
skyscraping view – lives crammed
like too many coats in a closet, front lawns
shrunk for turn lanes and bus-stops.

A woman in three-quarter length tweed
sighs over her seven dollar Starbucks,
the small called 'tall', as if it's a deal.
Overfilled cups take three hands to safely
snap lids, no room left for whipped cream,
even if we'd wanted it. Traipsing west,
our lids bubble over like hot mud-
springs, spotting our scarves.
You ask about things I've held back –
the way crowds hoard their distances.
I never could just disappear into anything.
In a chapel-sized record shop,
you help me find Jeff Buckley's *Grace*,
his haunting *Hallelujah* raising me

from rush hour's stop-and-go.
I hear he was in over his head,
like staring up from the street
to count glassy-eyed floors.

Throat Chakra

Still swaddled in sheets, I listen
through wafer-board walls,
my mother-in-law tottering
arthritically to the kitchen
in sloppy slippers, muttering to herself –
morning's many burdens.
She loses a stage-whisper debate
to her three cats cranky for breakfast,
sprinkle of kibble topping up their bowls.
Running tap, clanking stove-top –
her first pot of pekoe on the go.

Out of sync with the ceiling-fan thrum,
her daughter snores softly beside me,
more refined than her dad's
wood-lot rumble from the next room.
I stave off a sneeze –
morning pollens percolating
through the screen, but sleep abandons me.

I amble out to the kitchen.
She's so pleased someone else is up –
an audience for her running banter.
But it's too early, her words crowding me
out of the cottage and down
to the shore, where my Nescafe pairs
with seaweed and wet sand.
Strobes of diamond dust on the sunny waves,
swallows swooping for flies,
a lone cormorant crosses the cloudless sky.

Footsteps on the jetty –
my mother-in-law carrying another cup
of what she thinks I like in my coffee,
busy expounding on the day's beauty
and the flicker that followed her down here.
Now, I'm trapped at land's end
and it strikes me how her stiff upper lip
got her through the Blitz, helps her soldier on
with disc disease and diverticulitis,
always staying a step ahead
of self-doubt, never surrendering
to that quiet she fears
might one day drown her out.

A Bigger Room in Nirvana

I'd rather Buddha just showed me
the video of how things play out,
projected onto a towering curtain
of cumulous, a three-sixty degree
gossamer screen.

Maybe he'd let me lounge
a while in one of his lotus-blossom
armchairs, cradle my own weight
of being, pray a couple of
centuries might clear grief,
greed and bad air below.

Sure, a few more tours of
blood-and-bone might net me
a bigger room in Nirvana, but
what if it all shakes out the same:
Mike continues to achieve
below potential.

What I Need Is
Another Hole in the Head

Deliver me a line that flows
longer than five-minute epoxy,
tools smoother than silicone in the sun;
a metaphor that doesn't need tightening
like nearly every new sink's tail-piece, seeping
a smug drip or two, alliterations
too loath to let go.
Whipping up a batch of muscle and shiver
should be easier, like tinting paint.
But most days, writing is a storm of sawdust,
no glorious details appear, just tangled turns
of phrase and twisted greenstick breaks.
I might as well toss my words
into a cement-mixer. Maybe try
a good, medieval brain-letting
to exsanguinate
all my hang-ups, plug the hole
with plumber's putty and some trusty clichés.

Jesus Was Here

Feeding the donkeys, the boldest
ambles near, nostrils flaring, ears
as long as corn-cobs. She could have
been a star with those Hollywood lashes.
She stretches her neck to Guinness lengths,
nibbling the air until reaching my gift
of carrot. A thin black cross scribes
her back, stark on her storm-grey coat,
like Christ against the Golgotha sky.
Maybe they've only borne their stigmata
since Good Friday, branch broken
from the pre-Darwinian tree. Or maybe
Jesus just inked off each vertebra,
drawing his way into Jerusalem.

Untethered

What if my body isn't mine,
borrowed instead
from some rogue marionette
shaking off his strings?

Fuck the spectators,
soar through the side
of the circus tent,
hitch a ride
on the first southbound
to the Big Easy, find some
juke-joint to stir the dark in,
merge with flying fists,
voodoo grins,
unrepentant riffs.
Shadows sliding down the walls
like lacquer gone wild.

If Fried Eggs Were Tea Leaves

I strive to think good things
about the cracked and worn
vinyl seats. My coat stays on –

the ceiling vent a chilly
eavesdropper, cooling my coffee.
Despite cutting my fried eggs

down to size, nothing will stay
on my fork this morning.
Just another hopeless case of

white-bread surrender,
ketchup bleeding into oily shadows.
Maybe what I'm looking for

is already here, swirling
in the debris on my plate.
I recall how the frankness of

Carl Dennis laid bare to me
the necessity of always writing
honestly and now I regret

not being more attentive
when my grandmother taught me
to read tea leaves, how the truth

is invariably hidden
right in front of me.

On Not Visiting Cape Canaveral

It's not like I had my sights set
on outer space, shuttling up
into the great void to finally find
myself, another Major Tom.
One more check off the bucket list.
To stand there on NASA's historic turf
and gawk at the sheer enormity
of our need to leave home,
conquer
and come back again.

I hurtle on northwards,
two highway hours beyond
Orlando's Mickey-Mouse mania,
a blur of palmettos, fire-ant hills,
orange groves and horse farms.
The driver maneuvers around minivans,
big rigs and three helmetless bikers
still roaming the countryside after dawn.

My mother's winter retreat nestles
in a quiet park where there's free water,
grass-cutting and rumours
of alligators in the lake. But like UFOs,
hardly anyone here has seen them,
only done their part to pass along
the tale of a surly eight-footer
sunning itself on some-guy-named-Norm's dock.
I'll eventually wander over to see
the dock for myself, figuring if it exists
then other legends might still be out there.

The space shuttle could tweak its coordinates,
chase down the latest sighting of something
unexplained, see if NASA shares half as much
as this gated community's grapevine.
A day-trip to the Cape gets shot down,
too close to Daytona
and all that pre-race delirium.
I fly home with a vision
of I-75's green-sign promise
and the memory of smoky-white plumes
arcing across the TV screen
73 seconds after launch.

Talk Talk Talk

Is it such a stretch to think
we're born with a lifetime's
worth of chatter?
Prattle on too much in youth
and risk withering.
Too reticent? Stand aside
while Grandpa tells the world
why things were better
in his day – never did like turnips,
and where the hell
did he leave his shoes?

Consider the blurting sister-in-law,
overdrawn on her dowry of words,
loathe to let a thought simmer.
Uncle Doug falling asleep mid-
sentence like a gramophone
needle slowing to a slur.

I plod my way through parties,
slipping strategic *Holy shits*
into the bartender's
exhaustive account of his latest,
awesome snow machine;
sympathetic *tsks* for some-lady-
called-Donna's woeful tale
of her cousin's best friend,
whose neighbour's son-in-law
might have caught strep
from an unwashed peach;
or the repartee with my niece's
boyfriend: *Hey*, then
Hey.

Escape Hatch

My shoulders ache from pruning
shaggy trees, trimming surly
hedges. The table-saw screech
of cicadas across heat waves
like breaking-down Winnebagos.

Guilty once again of missing
who I used to be – suit and tie,
keyboard clatterer, a/c addict.
Coveted window seat, quarterly
reports, bottom lines.

Too soon, counting and
recounting the sides of
my pencil, imagining it
drawing a cartoon escape hatch
on the board room wall.

And now here I am, wishing I was
clean and dry and planted behind
a desk again, contorting brain instead
of body. Maybe it's the cat in me
wanting in, then wanting out, in and out,
waffling between worlds.

What if We Were All Morticians

and shared our loquacious notes
about polished pine boxes,
which brand of makeup brings out
a body's best, helps them look
most alive? We'd snicker over what hides
below the waist, draped away behind a
gathering of delicate, satin pleats:
maybe a wooden wedge propping up one hip
to a more aesthetic position,
a pair of polka-dot boxers, or empty
coffee cups and yesterday's folded news.

Convening for our weekly writing group,
we might be tempted to believe we're better
equipped than the rest of the living,
dissecting one another's work in our detached,
calculated way, sussing out each other's best
lines. Then we'd brainstorm: with or without
spectacles to frame images, cue up
metaphorical ascension; more stuffing
in sleeves to add muscle, bulking up
similes like cotton in cheeks.

But would we fear death any less, or just
differently? All too aware of what lies
in store, squirming at the thought of how
thoroughly our vessels will be drained
of every ethereal vision, eyelids
glued shut so no one will witness
our shock when we discover
it was always about the writing,
that last solitary word we heard,
buried in being alive.

Relevant

He could mull over Raymond Carver but
they've only just met, wax on about
Elizabeth Smart, but Grand Central's
too big of an echo. Al Purdy, Jack Gilbert,
Tony Hoagland, all fading from reach.

Maybe he's fading, too, nothing more
than the obsolete version of himself,
yet still preferring to cling to it
in the dark than lurch empty-
handed into the white expanse of day.

Sometimes, he goes so far as to feel
passed over by all that's faceless and new.
And the stalking shadow, a presence that abhors
small talk, resents his longing to connect,
become relevant once more, (or for once).

A simple chin-lift for his grieving would do.

He needs a fresh take on that boy inside
who quit speaking up for fear of being wrong
yet again, the tragic savvy of a 10-year-old
to know enough to sit up and shut up,
never voice how misunderstood he was.

And look at him now: divorced,
middle-aged, arthritic back, swapping
one derisive cliché for another. No longer
with a place to call his own, mired
in a quarter-rolling job, scribbling
sporadic words that might not surface –

or might.

Maybe Dean Young could help him
reinterpret what's real, Mark Doty beautify
the beasts of life and death, Louise Gluck
trace the curves of forgetfulness,
why what fades should fade.

Let Anne Michaels deliver him
some jewel from the flip-side of his
fogged-in horizon, help him to remember
why everything must have a name.

He Was Unhappy

Because nature is cruel in its beauty
and tomorrow can never be trusted.
Because the sun deemed him worthy
of a mere glimmer on its way to dusk.

Because he can't stop looking back,
because middle age is always too early.
Because his confidence died a slow, lingering
death and he still managed to miss the funeral.

Because he'll never read all the books
he owns and he used to mistake a lifetime
as forever. Because his best friend is sick,
yet often unfazed by death.

Because he has no certifications
but most days feels certifiable.
Because a failed marriage left him with nothing
to show for the years.

Because he can't afford his own
address, mired in his mother's basement.
Because what's left of his family is so broken,
he's only been able to deal with it in pieces.

Because 2AM can too often be an ordeal.
Because he's baffled to think
his spirit chose this for a comeback.
Because he dismisses his unhappiness

and repeatedly gets swindled by hope.
Because it's what he does best.

Exit Wounds

I could pretend I'm less alone.

Back to a long-ago kitchen,
bubbling pots, thumping cupboard doors,
whistling of the eternal kettle.
Chrome and Formica table,
(my favourite spot at the far end),
Tupperware leftovers, checkers and tea.

Now, upper cabinets' doors abducted,
wrenched from disfigured hinges.
Where the lowers once stood,
the flooring's lip curled into sneer,

exposing the bitter, black glare
of tongue-and-groove beneath,
decades taken for granted,
like the bones beneath my skin.

The stove is gone, revealing a supply cable
of contorted copper, cough of soot
smearing the wall around its exit wound.
Plunge a laced boot into wallpaper poppies,
plaster and lathe giving way, exhaling
a century's worth of rubble and grime.

Go ahead, fall over the brink –
you'll never feel more alive.

Black Birds

after André Kertész

Wires dissecting
overcast sky, only one
claimed. Like a blocked
third chakra, crows lined up
and looming heavy-
hearted overhead, waiting –
all 13 of you – for me to
make a move. Are you
regrets, omens or
nothing more than black birds?
Can a wrong choice
still be the right way?

My sense of self
like bared stone, carved
pagoda-like, erosion
of the years, absorbing
rain, deflecting sun.
Come down from your stand,
relieve me
of your shadows, choose
a more fitting perch
on a limb of ash,
release my smouldering
to the waking world.

Trust

If asked your intentions,
shrug slowly.
It's true you've always known.

If summoned to the temple
consider devotion, brothers
taunting you
like snapping prayer flags.

Silhouette of a solitary crow.
Trust the feather left behind.

If it embitters you – release
the ballast. If it shouts
in your face – bless it
with Zen and grit.

Ars Poetica

I should dye my hair blonde and move to Whistler.
I should dig seven holes in my yard, despair when I only catch six meteorites.
I should hang someone else's clothes on the line.
I should call a random stranger's number, tell them to quit bothering me.
I should dye my hair brown and move back from Whistler.
I should break all my pencils, swear off any further mistakes.
I should be getting an act together.
I should burn another CD of someone else I'll never listen to.
I should sleep with my head at the foot of the bed, see if I wake up changed.
I should break with tradition and start enjoying myself.
I should break with tradition and stop repeating myself.
I should break some new habits.
I should buy a pair of $100 jeans, help me look like I'm worth it.
I should shave my head and blind the sun.
I should learn how to harmonize.
I should order the Test Pattern channel for late nights.
I should stow away to Tijuana, insisting I'd only nipped out for milk.
I should grow a set of wings, stash them in the trunk for emergencies.
I should order a spare spine.
I should argue with myself out loud.
I should be more vigilant.
I should scream on Thursday afternoons.
I should make a point of meeting up with the real me.

You Are Happy

Remember when you used to wear a watch?
Before you strapped 10,000 steps to your wrist
and your pocket started chirping with texts.

Before bark began to peel from the lofty
crimson-king centerpiece in your front yard,
and rust appeared around your vanity's drain.

Never mind. Straight back to the dealer –
there's another smudge on your
limited edition Lexus and its opalescent finish.

Upgrade your windows before the neighbours notice
they're lowly crank-outs, not double-hung and
triple-glazed. Get that cedar mulch
absurdly mounded around every honey locust

because *Better Homes and Gardens* said so.
Purchase only artisanal potato chips – twice the price,
gluten-free, and everyone will be impressed.

Maybe even you. A persona only fully realized
with the walk-in closet you had to wait until
you were forty to find and fill. Now picture yourself
robbed of all the brand names and prestige:

no more nine-foot ceilings, three-car garage,
grand piano, in-ground pool. What's left?
Nothing more than me. *Ch-ching*.

Yellow

He is the only man in a yellow shirt,
a shade too bright
for the hospital's lofty atrium,
maybe too close to caution.

Nurses scrubbed in royal blue
thread through the milling
of the dazed and bruised
like rivulets of rush.

He has stumbled into a state
of beacon, a reluctant boulder
caught up in rapids. His is the yellow
of police-tape, of small steps,

of daffodils and dahlias,
of urine and infection; the ability to
stand up and stand out, to accept
being stared at, the right to remain alone.

A black knapsack is slung
over his shoulder, clings to him
as he swings into Pre-Admission's
waiting room. Along with the requisite

water and tide-you-over granola bars,
he carries a David Kirby collection
of poetry that might help deflect
a sloppy brunette's relentless banter

one row over. But even his shirt
can't shut her out. Doctors
come and go, decked in lab coats
and clipboards, all the props.

Pleased to meet you, they insist
to each successive patient;
Right this way coming off as
nothing more than rote.

Returning to the atrium, he finally spots
the shirt's lone sign of solidarity:
a *Wet Floor* sandwich board
pleading for recognition

near the centre of the terrazzo expanse.
The Information Desk's silver-on-blue
refuses to get involved, but he knows
it's there. The back of his neck is breezy

and bare, the vulnerability of a v-neck.
It's the one part of him that itches
to jump on the food court's condiment counter,
demand a better-priced corned beef special

and howl.

Acknowledgements

A huge thank you to Don Gutteridge for selecting my manuscript as an Honourable Mention in the inaugural 2021 Don Gutteridge Poetry Award Contest, and equally to Richard Grove and Wet Ink Books.

I am grateful to the editors of the following literary magazines for first publishing earlier versions of some of these poems: *The Antigonish Review*, *The Dalhousie Review*, *Event*, *Existere*, *The Fiddlehead*, *Freefall*, *The New Quarterly*, *untethered*, *The White Wall Review* and *The Windsor Review*. The poem 'What I Need is Another Hole in the Head' was shortlisted for *Freefall's* 2019-'20 Annual Poetry Contest.

The italics in the poem 'Alive' are from Dallas Green's 'Day-Old Hate.'

Many thanks to my writing group compatriots, past and present, for all their help: Mollie Coles Tonn, Jacquie Dawe, Brian Dundas, Carol Gall, Jaclyn Guildemond, Glenn Hayes, Heida Norberg, Denise Raike, Elaine Rodaro, Richard Rodaro and Sharon Wilston.

And to my fellow writers at Los Parronales, near Santiago, Chile, for their collective muse and inspiration, during our two-week retreat in January, 2009, led by Barry Dempster: Cynthia French, Carol Gall, Elizabeth Greene, Ruth Roach Pierson, Mel Sarnese and Susan Siddeley.

Hugs for my mother Phyllis and brother Steve, who patiently watched this book come to life.

All my love to Lisa for turning me back around to feel the sun on my face.

Many thanks to Karen Dempster for her undying support, keen ear, and many delicious meals.

Much appreciation to those individuals whose paths have crossed mine in various ways, and whose encouragement will not be forgotten: Dennis Bouwman, Linda Burkhardt, Rejeanne Burkhardt, Vivian Campbell, Yvonne Coon, Kathy Fleming, Peter Katz, John and Mary Shirtliff, Cathy Summers, Brian Vanderlip and Ed and Janet Vandermolen.

Finally, my endless gratitude to Barry Dempster for his insight, compassion and commitment. His ability to adroitly dismantle my writing's armour to let the light shine through has been a joy to behold; his unconditional friendship a gift from the gods.

Author Statement

Even as a child, I penned little stories, but never seriously pursued writing, (beyond typical high school scribbles of teenage angst), until I was close to 40. Spotting an ad in my local newspaper for a night school writing course, I impulsively registered. My teacher proved to be the celebrated poet Barry Dempster, who introduced me to the world of poetry, eventually becoming an invaluable mentor and, more importantly, a true friend.

My relationship with writing has always been hot and cold. Anxiety and depression often fuel a negative voice that, more than once, has nearly convinced me to put away the pen for good. But invariably, Barry nudges me back to the page.

Growing up, I remember my parents being very driven, weekends always abuzz with housework, yard work and car maintenance. I inherited their house pride, but have always strived to be less strict with myself, aware of the value of a healthy work-play balance.

My biggest influence was my father, Ron Madill. He was well-read, eloquent and sarcastic, (all qualities I admire), and when I recall now his knowledge of all things hands-on, it still astounds me. I would also say my friend, John Shirtliff, who shared a similar work ethic to my dad, and had a wisdom far beyond his abbreviated school years. Finally, my dear friend Barry Dempster, whose incredible talent in both writing and teaching has been a gift, and his relentless tenacity throughout his own personal challenges a true inspiration.

A Short Author Bio

When not writing, Mike Madill pursues freelance editing, and has also taken turns as a social worker, computer analyst and home contractor. He holds a B.A. in Psychology from York University.

His poems have been published across Canada, including in *The Antigonish Review, The Dalhousie Review, Event, Existere, The Fiddlehead, Freefall, The Nashwaak Review, The New Quarterly, untethered, Vallum, White Wall Review* and *The Windsor Review.* He was shortlisted for *Freefall's* 2019-20 Poetry Contest, and an Honourable Mention in the inaugural 2021 Don Gutteridge Poetry Award Contest earned him publication of his debut collection, *The Better Part of Some Time.*

www.ingramcontent.com/pod-product-compliance
Lightning Source LLC
Chambersburg PA
CBHW030222140626
46545CB00012B/2619